He Looked Beyond My Faults and Saw My Needs

He Looked Beyond My Faults and Saw My Needs

Leonard Gontarek

Hanging Loose Press
Brooklyn, New York

Published by Hanging Loose Press, 231 Wyckoff Street, Brooklyn, NY 11217-2208. All rights reserved. No part of this book may be reproduced without the publisher's written permission, except for brief quotations in reviews.

www.hangingloosepress.com

Printed in the United States of America
10 9 8 7 6 5 4 3 2 1

Hanging Loose Press thanks the Literature Program of the New York State Council on the Arts for a grant in support of the publication of this book.

Cover art by Leonard Gontarek

Cover design by Marie Carter

ISBN: 978-1-934909-31-7

Library of Congress cataloguing-in-publication available on request.

for Stephen Berg

CONTENTS

Ouzo

Airports And Trees

Strange Days

Mystery

In America

Summer Day

1. Ouzo

Autumn Sonata

Jackson Pollock was afloat in his life
with a view of burning cruise ships,
which was the world, if that makes sense,
and I understand if it doesn't.

I think of Pollock when I am walking the edge
of a field in autumn imprinted with shadows
of leaves, and lit leaves among the dark aspects.
I connect the calm to Pollock,
strangely, you might think.

Pollock once sat in a field with an elixir,
after selling his soul to the devil.
A mixture of whiskey and dusk.
It looked like the glass was frothing,
but it was ordinary mist.

Recently I looked at a Pollock painting,
which, always sacred to me,
looked like a bunch of paint piled on a canvas.
One of the saddest afternoons.

HUNGER

I have been laid off from Poetry.

I beg on the street. Can you   help me   get some   food?
No, not money, do my shopping, I hate shopping.

Twilight makes a fence along the cemetery.

In window of music store, they've built a house of cards
from Philip Glass' new CD, *Music For Cleaning Apartments*.

It starts to snow.

FOR NOW

after Machado

The earth is red. Spears descend from the moon as in a child's painting.

Stars turn to stars blurred in the river. There is, in me, sadness separated from joy.

Gold window by gold window, I think Philadelphia

has been given up to the darkness, branching street by branching street.

Late October

Traffic slurs into Indian summer. The class is taking out its papers. Trees rustling.

A wheelbarrow flares with death. Crabapple smeared with death. I must go, I
    must go, I think.

The squeaking of crows irritates me. The scent of rhododendron, too heavy.

I must go, five years in the future my food is prepared and waiting at
    The Silver Lotus.

The flies are already tired of swimming in the won ton.

AUTUMN IN THE WORLD

Maybe not God, but religion, between Little Pete's Diner
and the corner of Pine and Quince as leaves fly.

A kid takes a stick to the branches and
blackbirds land.

I am looking for an opening to come to know
with my tongue. I undo your hair. Here the analogy breaks down.

The line is long at Dante's Ribs. The leaves exquisite, combust.
A fly lands on the heart. Evening follows.

Hymn

I have been a poet for 25 years.

I am stepping out, just now, for stamps.

Terrorists pull up in a silver Mercedes—

the newer, American model—spray Uzis in my direction.

I fall to the ground, riddled with doubt.

Redemption / Salvation

A man wanted to write a poem. In it, scent of peeled logs

and oranges. Rimbaud on his deathbed. Window, open.

The Father of Modern Poetry is 37, and dying, motions the man

closer: Don't forget to water my cats. Whispers.

December

The songs are right, we have to get through.

Trees, nests of mist, the early part, the first two months.

Put your hand on the back of my neck, cradle me to you.

In the meantime, this what we are

bequeathed: blackbirds stropping the branches.

April

You introduced me to ouzo.
If you sprinkled a few drops
of water in the clear liquor,

it turned smoky. Remember?
Afterward we were drunk enough to make love.
A gray day with white and pink blossoms in the trees.

2. Airports And Trees

Outline

Perhaps it is all curfew, squawking crows.
Small paper anchors lowered into fall.
The darkness, bushes turn to mist, to fire.
Frail is such a heart. Without merit.

The gift is layered. A bounty, a
remarkable, annotated myth.
Melancholy is fair. I tremble in what I don't know.
Father, this is no elegy.

The children sit in rows in fall.
Praying mantises in palms of their hands.
They do not flicker like small, transparent flames.
The Interior is important and is made

important by the leaves, tapping,
picking over one another.
We approve. We look from the window and approve.

Imago Mundi

There was the wolf that ate his leg, then his other one.
Then ate all of him. You would think sorrow would disappear too.
But apparently that is not how it works. *Earth to Leonard.*
What works: So hot, the flowers have melted.
But not you, who look from a distance like a peaceful Kevin Kline.

I love that it can all be placed in a reliquary. I love the Egyptian writing.
It is Egyptian. I love that it can be catalogued.
I love the picture I have of everything.
It's a map, of sorts, blackened, soupy lettuce. Pick out
the eyes, that is, olives, and you will have the phoenix.

I could talk about the fire, Pain. But that would be
inelegant of me. Love has turned love salmon, blood red
ink running in between. *Earth to Leonard.*
Move along, there's nothing to see here.
It's mysterious. A real gate in a painted field.

APPRENTICESHIP

See how the rain & screens form a way to you.
It is not just that the way is lit by brilliant maples.
It is more than that. In the reserve of dark,
we are happy to be pained by love & mysteries,

so meaning may elude us. Oblivion, blissfully so.
All night long. God fingers us, all night long.
Cars skirl the wet streets. Brilliant red cars.
Leaves don't so much fall, as

are dumped into wet needles.
Difficult to tell dream from the other thing.
Inhabit this world when I damn well feel like it.
Compassion is not a requirement. Mystery makes

matters worse & my shadow is small, affectionate,
wiry.

Loop

The trees are infinite. A particle of bird sits on a branch.

The clouds, scum-caked bottoms of boats.

Heart, dog on a 20-foot leash, awake & restless, goes just so far.

Praise, infinite. The trees have made us for themselves.

I want to know death, smear of red, understand.

Cardinal hidden in the leaves, baby in the barn.

Cologne of undertaker, standing among flowers, not pleased until it comes to us.

Clouds hanging from the branches, cats, from the branches.

Fat black crows secured in their teeth.

False spring, manifold. My faith is little. Tenderness, infinite.

Poison arrives as postcard. Part of letter that you lick.

God is shaken out, powder in secret compartment of the ring.

On Earth

A crow sits on the cross of a telephone pole.

Dragonflies fighting over air,

even here on the floor of hell, a

punky crumbling mess rich with

fragrant disappearing flowers I do

not know the names of.

I think of our disputes over sex.

Scentless sting of kiss afterward.

Irritating traffic, cicadas.

Shirring backroads leading past a porch

of inbred moonshiners one

marvelously tipsy Zen monk,

prisoner of cypress trees and his shyness.

Loop

I stood before a painting called *Kneel.*

I stood before a painting called *The Greek Word For Air*. Gold.

The world is Sacred. Female is water, voyage, arrival.

Male is gold. Interesting, let me see if I understand you.

The idol is not created out of necessity.

The idol is created, then its reason is invented

& that makes you god? Isn't a discussion of the object

& the fact that it may not exist a kind of prayer?

Doesn't prayer make your head ache like a too-fast cold substance?

The world is Sacred. I have a little feather-thing in my hair.

The world is prayer & gold & the blue of Cezanne's fruit,

chalk that rubs off on a teacher's coat.

Right there under the sign that says *Exit*, people enter anyway.

So many and so quickly they blur & turn into the light

of a peaceful summer day, in strips across God's huge odd-scented lap.

063

I take the bread. I set down the heart. Through a small opening in
   morning, crows.

A bucket whistles past. I have a mouthful of night. The leaves, spot-lit.
   As you wish. As you vanish.

Who led Germany during the Second World War? Hands shoot in the air.
   All dying to be right.

The Revolutionaries are at the entrance of the church, testing the temperature
   of the holy water.

I breathe in a world of water and leaves. Leaves being raked. Tables being
   wiped. Filled in by furious late morning light.

Thick trees where we are rerouted by nightfall.

The funeral director on our street is rinsing silverware. His first date in years.

If you scrape the walls, there may be enough to get high.

Here at the end of the world: hydrangea, blue grass, on television.

How about some advice for me, the King of Wishes: *Do not seek, do not
   condemn yourself.*

On nights like these, sleek and black, the seeds rattle inside the hands.

The light is a door, large, open, brighter than the rest.

VOICE

Shipwrecked clipper ship clouds

A horse scratching his ass on the corner of post-expressionist canvas

Will there be perfume in the afterlife

with names like *Inflorescence, Possession, Testament?*

it is, in the gunburst

it is, in the *stolen into,*

in the mouth of night, in the man praying for weeds,

a lubricant,

plum olive sky

wickling, exact, seeped shadow

light travels, light touches

Grand life, the hour guided by clouds

Falling

The poem's father is a drunk.
The poem's mother becomes cold-hearted.
The poem reads as translation.
It begins the first
of many affairs.

Snow is falling
off the roof.

The crows are beautiful,
serrate the dark,
which is beautiful,
with their flight,
just after dusk.

I'm empty,
too, you know,
I'm nothing
but a whore
of dusk.

The Summer

It worries me, the weather.
The impatiens fold up.

I can see, on the glass, my breath.
One hundred degrees.

Nothing to do, but finish
my Absolut, keep to myself.

Take in a show. Nightclub
gone to seed. Erotic act:

Leda And The Swan. Leda,
of course, a woman. The swan,

not necessarily a man.
Try not to look at the others,

on the way in, and out.

ORPHEUS IN HIS UNDERWEAR

Two beers in front of him. He drinks the warm one.
Vodka he bought for the blue bottle's drawing of a castle.
Eurydice he is thinking of.
How she turned around to lock eyes when he humped her from behind.
He shouldn't tell you that. But, it's done.
Michael Douglas DVD on with sound off.
I loved that bitch. How someone discloses they love orange chicken.
The river smells chemical, meaning the river of death.
Eurydice Disappears made the headlines.
A month later, banished to page 5.
Then it vanished, reappearing as an item on the anniversary.
Fucking vodka. This movie makes no sense.

EMAIL

Pain is under the skin, scum, floating bugs. Peeled back:
clear pond, moon, small as lump.
Head deep in lap, I see only your hair.

I hold your foot in my hand, nails polished pink.
Touch wrist at breakfast, with one finger.

Inhale green tea, opening a well.
Scarves still tied to bedposts.

Fish mouth on glass, I want to hook on to you.
Lick lips, plate clean. Afterward, I want you.
Outside of us, darkness, restaurant on fire in fine rain.

So what if their art is naive, they paint what is.
I see moon, crescent, halo of the rest, between your legs.
Admit it makes you wet.

I roll down your violet underpants, you go off to work.
All day, tang of money, skin, drip at back of throat like allergies.

Pitcher, beaded, pewter and beaded.
Lost, I become distracted by detail.
Your husband and children on lawn.
At the window behind them, you open your robe.

Out of everything, the dark, fireflies.
Train whistle, tobacco smoke, devour the night.
Hair fanned out on my thigh.

The cat is very interested in my lips and face.
I suspect she likes the scent of what I've eaten.

Afterward, I go to hell like a bullet from a sad man.
Beautiful nude women, trees, along the way.
Take off my clothes, you said, *so they tear.*

The Hills

Dark drops on creek running with
trout & tenderness, directly to your plate,

elaborate: with leaves, raspberries, grapes.
She is pressed naked against the hotel window.

Believe me, it is what she wanted.
On a high floor, what number I don't remember,

but an unimpeded view of the city.
She swears she does not remember biting me.

I thrust.
She lifts to the tip of her toes.

I know this is strange,
but there are many things about that day that were strange.

AIRPORTS AND TREES

He adds cream
to the coffee in the dream,
which ordinarily he doesn't do.

She thought when he removed his tongue
from her, it was over,
but only the quiet was over.

After a week loving my woman,
I am a terrorist.

I would buy you a dress
I would rip from you,
if that is what you want.

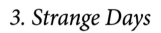

3. Strange Days

September Evenings

Kids cross the path of the car in my sleep,
chasing a ball at the sharp curve near the Bible camp, into the woods.
The car is white and the trees are turning.
I get out, get down on my knees, pray for silence.

Light piles like needles, sizzles. Ah, but it is gold coming through branches.
We have heard so much about the field. Entering it, it lets us in.

You are doing it wrong, he tells me. How can you fish wrong?
You are doing it all wrong. Cumulus scrapes the lake. Teenage girls snap
        pictures of it.
Fragrant as orange, the clouds are sorrow. A woman sunbathing.
        Sorrow, too, the water.

Many ask me about the nature of dying. One I have drinks with,
who selects a tie and jacket for me. Summer is ending. I slow down
        and let the deer pass.

Light breaks, plaster drifts from trees. Low wall dividing the field from the field.
Hastily made signs reading: *Wet Paint, Metamorphosis, Symbolism, Romance,*
placed in the dark roses. Look, the angle of the roof, moving up
        the morning glories, lengthens.

Larvae have attached to the branches. A lacework of white worms
        eating at the leaves.
The residents have come to accept it. Some with exact netting
        covering their faces.

Like your heart beating in a jar on your dresser. Is that what it is like?
Someone dressed as a funeral director dropping a hand in your lap
        in a movie theater.
Isn't that what it's like?

He wears a crown fashioned from found objects and foil. You've seen
        him, haven't you?
How many people wearing crowns do you see on the street, that
        you would care to admit?
I saw him in the mountains, crossing a road. I drove through him. Each
        morning was the same.
Each morning gold light sizzled through the trees, hissed in the grass.

In room of soft nudes. Floors, quiet, coated with scarlet dust. After hours.
Painting of peaceful town, underwater. The children are trying to
        tell us something.
Bubbles come from their mouths. Gold square at the bottom reads:
        Lake Village, Artist Unknown.
What we know, what we do not know, difficult.

The planet is holy, I am told. Iridescent, the pigeons twirl into the trees.
North, a man sits on a porch, surrounded by maples, one branch
        starting to orange.
He juggles sorrow and joy. Sorrow, he observes, settles like pond water in a glass.
Dusk, the water going out. A gold square at the bottom reads:
The Floors Are Quiet, Coated With Scarlet Dust.

The light falling into the street, from the trees, the flowers that are late and cool,
        go to the heart.
The mist that seeps from the mountains above The Lake of Clouds, the silver line
        of funeral cars,
oranges in the hearse, go to the heart. Gold and dark stripes across the grass
go to the heart. Petulant drip of the fountain, larks breaking from the branches,
        go to the heart.

Our neighbors sit in the great shadow of a tree. They cannot put it into words.
We cannot put it into words, they say. I walk a line of trees.
These are strange days with good signs. Clouds—huge, orange and silver,
        liquid, race past.

Miniature II

Leaked shadow, dripped leaves. Rich shadow.
Deer wandering from their thrones.
Skywriting in stunning
AM. Don't know it can't be done through slogans
lifted from Lankavatara, translated. God is lost
in gold key. Red shadow, sheet used for
target practice. Buddha wants a puppy, it's me.
Pathetic confetti on return to paradise. Rain, silvered.
End of the world. Bomb skittered loose. I remove
honey from you. Prayer is papery, cinnamon.
Why the hood, why the dead? I say I am
shepherd. Drugged flock. Wandered off, stuff I can't recall.
Given, ate, sold, betrayed, traded, can't say.
Interesting robe. Rain a lemonade. Necklace soaks
in. In. In house. In bird. Crisis.
1) The love of the bird for the metal bird
2) The love of the stain in the grass,
   loneliness, for the identical, Lord,
   smaller & smaller a) this is no different
   b) there is the object & what it contains
   i.e., the Real is merely nearby. So why does
   she weep & her tears grow tiny. She floats
   down the slope they have cut away for power lines.
   Her hair sparks, as do the tips of branches
   where they drag the ground.
3) Not merely,
   but rising above it: ghost second object.
   God lost like a key. Rain lowers,
   stronger apples drop. Healed shadows, slipped leaves,
   shadowed blue.
4) Always is crucial, key:
   such as the leaves throb & wonder & wipe chalk
   dust on themselves. The harsh word for
   hold spelled on the wall. So small, false, tenderly clustered.

Twenty Lines For j

You have to understand, I use the window to leave the landscape.

The light either covers me, or walks alongside in my shape.

I am Sebastien walking down the street, strolling, riddled with confusion.

You have to understand, it seemed strange. You would have to admit it was like a
daffodil, turned down & tied.

You have to understand, I am obsessed, I am *what chair?* I eat *what chair?*

I lie in bed, eye open.

The light either covers me, or climbs the slope to escape.

You have to admit, like a thunderbolt, tooth & nail, terrible, turned dove.

Or is it God I am thinking of? I should know, I am wearing his cloak.

You have to understand, I wanted to be an undertaker, so I (dreamed) painted one.

I married one. Gold of paints. I wanted to describe the sheen of her suit.
The worn, the silver. Aura, I drew the self.

There were 4 titles & trees. Just as quickly, 144. I was afraid to look.

You have to understand, it was snowing, it is still snowing.

My skin gave off a green & blue glow. Blue & violet. Bad meat. *Mal.*

You have to understand, I tried to give them what they wanted.

Did I? I don't remember. We ate. The food made crunching sounds like ice.

Was I happy? I don't know. I walked into the hills with a book that disappeared
in summer.

errata Lines 15-17 should read:

The dog barks *arp, arp,* at the tin can lid moon.

Abstraction migrates in the dark, new, unmarked vans.

She was nude & played the accordion, made me sad, melancholy, aroused.

I am happy. Rooms have no names. The picture, get it. Eurydice wasn't that soft
to begin with.

Light is rubric. It's central to this. Neither the stars nor the glitter care for me.

I am writing my name, fast, on a blackboard. The years going out, one at a time,
like lights in the building. I'm happy, you understand.

Dirt Floor II

In the trees, this balcony. The light in things. Lime drink. The panes of sky cut
 through us.
small souls. Congregated gnats in my dream, my movie. Fireflies I inhale.
 changes I have feared.
When will I come back. When will I come to love it. I long for Night + lantern.
Beautiful enough. To call this Lantern. Beautiful enough. Lantern this,
 lantern that.
Make my own with the shiniest one. Abstract dusk. Throws a kind of shade.
Deeper into the words, on the faces of the passengers. No train, but look. How
explain this jolting, this scent of humans, brushing against them when it is
 not what is meant.
I want these things as I understand. Causing images to blend, erased edge.
& I want these things. Death will clip our wings with pinking shears, moreover.
A pleasure not unlike pepper & chocolate. Moreover, branches & leaves float,
discordant, clouded light, outbreak of water. I fear dreams & memories
 in a junkyard.
There was
a woman who did not love me, whom I loved. I went down to the river, laying
 down my crown,
waded in. *Must be drunk.* The light is everything: amulet, scapula, snowglobe
 of New York City.
How could it not be about the wind in the tops of trees (like sea), darkening
 sky. This last Saturday
in September. The man mowing two stories below. The happiest man on earth,
 for some reason. Each
curve
he mows, followed by a darker one. We are for the light. Death courses shiny
 blood (like questions)
(& commas). A small wheel from a toy in childhood. A compact your mother
 gave you. You
remember that day, the weather. I opened a book, yesterday. I believe a small
 page slid from it.

WORST ENEMY

There have always been too many trees.
I smell death across the silver water.
Residue on the iridescent shore.
No one will pole me there.
I dislike rain. I have never liked it.
You may think otherwise from previous statements.
It should be light, but it is dark.
It will stay this shade of dark all day.
When the deer lick me, their tongues are rough
and part of me disappears.
The morning following battle, the mist burns off.
The flowers sizzle and the small lungs
of birds are bursting with poison.
Music was background noise.
I could have done without most of it.
I would have done anything to keep
the child hidden in the barn alive.
Gold sticks of light are mixed with the
straw and those that come through the door are blurred light.
I came in peace, that much I know.

INCOMING PRAYER

I told the woman in the garden, Autumn is without birds,
as if she didn't know.
The leaves, a Persian carpet.
She kissed me during the war.

During the war, she said,
we hid under everything. We hid under each other.
Sometimes, nothing happened. The planes kept going,
transporting a strange cargo, bodies packed in ice and oranges.

4. Mystery

NOTEBOOK

I help apply her lipstick. I draw them twice their size.
Someone has dunced a statue with an orange danger cone.
The area around the fountain in three inches of shadow.
I wet my finger more than necessary & turn a page of *The Odyssey*

Iris petals lean & fall into shadows. I long for differently.
You must know I give something to those who beg for it.
Something dropping in the night. I am not happy. I am at home.
Changing amounts of light through the branches. I want to give you a picture.

The circles on the bar, none complete, disappear. Mist, this morning,
      Indian summer.

Angels sway to their music, eyes closed, like high-schoolers with headphones.

But I can't complain, angels, nonetheless. The dog barks. God barks more.

NOTEBOOK V

The angel asks if we have thought things over. Close, her perfume on you.
God watches on TV.

Karma ran over my dogma.
Vodka, cocaine, *Gap* cologne cocktail.

Do I know what I mean? My sister in any windy
garden, cupping a praying mantis like a green flame.

The Buddha hears all prayers with his big ears. *buddha error.*

Goddamn Sacre Coeur is everywhere.

The trees begin.
Night, commuted to morning.

Me, I miss everything. I have my nose buried,
so to speak, in Madame Bovary the whole trip.

Highlighting, with a
black magic marker,
The Secrets of Zen.

God, truth, hate, envy, thanks, I'm full.

I fly in my dreams. It is consoling.

The world calls me *momma.*

I wait for the rusty factory gate to open. Drinking in dawn, pitching woo
to archangels.

The firetruck rushes, sad dirty faces crunching distorted chocolate rabbits,
weeping. O how I long for the time just before dark.

Reading Circle Jerk

My neighbor's weed whacker goes gold. I like the irony, melting, in late
    afternoon light.
I'm knocking back shots of tequila & tonic. He's snapping off chicken heads
    with an ax,
vacuuming leaves with his other hand. Should I pay attention? Butterflies &
    moths lift into the trees.
I'm reading Proust. I'm leafing through Marquez' stuff. Do I believe it?
I'm up to page 139 of a Chandler novel. You know, where the equivalent of
    the blonde goddess
who is *trouble* but can't spell it (& I trust about as far as I can throw my car),
    distractedly enters,
creaking like plastic upholstery. Simultaneously, my son decides this is a good
    time to quietly
blow up a brown paper bag & explode it. Laugh, go ahead, he's gunning
    for you too.
How *Ulysses* ends, I can't say. No, I can't say. No I can't. Isabella, my calico,
settles in the tenderness of low lamp & my lap. Morning is a movie
    in her memory,
with its fragrance of wharves & woodsmoke. Are those two nude women,
    coiled
across the alley, trying to tell me something? One, reading a book whose title
    I can't make out,
a gelatin nude photograph on the jacket. The other, white-knuckling a copy
    of *Mein Kampf,*
absentmindedly tracing a pink aureole with her free hand. I love the odor of
    pages, new & yellowed equally.

Two Philosophical Models

one

And I find a note in my meatloaf:
I don't want to be looked at by men,
I want to be felt by their hands.
I look around the restaurant. All of

the women, beautiful and smiling.
I think I have discovered Meaning.
The waitress wakes me from my reverie:
It is starting to rain, maybe

you should bring the baby in.

two

It was unusual, he had nothing to say.
God it was unusual, it seemed unusual.
After all, he was Wallace Stevens.
His thoughts were unfinished.

Some were just titles:
A Lecture On Philosophy. A Lecture On Poetry.
A Lecture On Seashells.
He wandered around the subjects,

a man with a perfect speech in his head
who through deep psychological fear
never gets around to asking the woman out.

Abruptly, he announced the reading over:
I guess I'll be taking off now.
His words, *taking off*,
making sounds like a motor starting and engaging,

spreading out his arms,
running down the aisle.

MYSTERY

Emily Dickinson didn't leave her house for 32 years.
I'm not so sure. Didn't the neighborhood boys taunt her?
try to lure her out, because they were, you know, boys.
Hey Emily, your poetry sucks! Emily Dickinson is a hermit crab!

What happens after the dark is doused? It's still dark in the Dickinson house!
Miss Dickinson sleeps with the delivery boy!
Didn't she storm out the door, rush down the steps
as they scattered like cats, and find herself, broom in hand, in the backyard,

and think, as evening cooled, the first star surfaced,
leaves trembling,
"This isn't what I thought at all, contrariwise, this is rather nice."
Didn't they, huh, didn't they?

Complete Zen Writings

Zen Story

A frog sat on the ledge of a tall building.
A crowd gathered. Someone yelled, *Jump.*

Haiku

Honey,
You drive like a
Zen koan.

Taoist Story

Lao Tzu returned, in a dream. *I never said,
It's raining, let's have a picnic,* he said.

Haiku

Mosquitoes
I Ching

The Poems of the Late T'ang

They're still
Not here

Zen Story

In a diner, I order scrambled eggs
And a chicken salad sandwich,
To see which comes first.

Haiku

Two fat sparrows.
Two fat worms.
Peaceful evening.

5. In America

Study / Field

Light flows from the
field, the field spilling
after that. It's hard
to say.
When you introduce

light, leaves, a little wind,
the self, the difficulty
is trying to gather
everything in. A woman
coming from the yard,

fragrant with laundry.
Out of sorts.
A deer,
where there wasn't
one.

Study / Bees

Sound of rain, room catching fire. When speaking with a woman

you should get close enough to breathe her perfume, as I have.

Vague trees, coiled gauze. I must know more than I let on.

September. Orange elms bleeding bees. White gull unscrolls.

Gold clasp catches in throat. Laden with autumn, summer water,

black leaves on leaves. The lake pearls & I swim to you.

Study / Leaves

If I follow & I think I'm starting to, the world is a plaza,

large, marble, littered with yellow leaves, bright against the overcast

& I am King of Autumn. Beyond the door is hell, where the leaves burn.

Beyond that birds tossing as in a dryer. Two women trail their hair over me.

Star barrettes. Sticks, leaves. Petals. Swept neat as campsite.

Ah, the sweeping, the blessed sweeping. Heart knocks like radiator pipe.

Study / Moon

It's interesting, he flares a match to look at a star chart.

It's interesting, the image is thrown back into the dark. A twig snap, just as expected.

A voice, stern & fatherly, hushes the extras, or has he just imagined it.

Moon, cylindrical-shaped in pond. Everything heightened in crosshairs of God.

Study / Violet

The snow that appears violet, later, in a photo,
now lights up all of the night.
Dark is not an enigma. We are the enigma.
We carry the moon from the well

to the door of the house.
Evil is made to sit in the corner, silent.
A child. Milk. It spills across the floor, moonlight.
The cat licks up the truth, fast as it can. The cat loves the child.

STUDY / SCARLET

In the story, two men make love to you simultaneously.

Their tans, artificial, apricot. You are punished for this.

Tied to a tree & whipped. How dreams are like old movies.

In the story you pore over miniature paintings. Autumn decants from the trees.

If you think about it, the world is made up of little stories.

Pond, dark, inlaid with gold & scarlet leaves.

LANDSCAPE

Through hill of trees, cloud shadow followed.

A hole in God, light fell into the trees, wet with light.

The world changed, while everything changed.

POEM 2

God have a little luck. God have a little heart.

God have a little fear. A sky that come down.

Field of milkweed and cow. Girl that leave him.

Girl that tell him why. Thing to locate stars with.

Don't need it. Two fingers of whiskey.

More 'cause ice melted. God have the rest.

ESCAPING IN AMERICA

Is your logic correct? You are running out of gas, so you speed up.
You notice the boys blurred in a yard, looking up, a ball
floating above them. Becoming dark. The sign you prayed for:
Mobil Station Open All Night. Wind out of view,
from sea, pines. The attendant wipes his
nose on the rag he used to wipe oil stick. God certainly in the trees.

Rain Early in September

I don't make much of it,

they are words spoken in a dream, and God is a dream.

Untitled

Rimbaud is lying with me in hell. My lover between us.
Such are the dreams in heat. A milk truck blows

through the street. There are no orders. The driver, ashen,
distant, when he speaks. If at all.

Bringing with him cooler weather, revived violets? No.
We are tiny and the oven is turned up higher.

HELL

With one hand I am spooning *Trix* to myself,
with the other I am putting the man next to me into the past tense with a pistol,
with the other I am turning the pages of *Being and Nothingness*, for eternity .

ETUDE 3

When mysteries fall apart & float into the world, it enriches the world.
Catbird hopped-up on chitchat (eccentric as it is) & twilight.
The clouds rule the pond. Ever, fishermen negotiate them.

What is that cologne you are wearing? You smell like a cheap funeral home.
Summer is building an ark & a coffin & a cage for crickets.
Love the leaves & silver maples.

Given that, they will descend on you like beautiful handwritten letters
from God's diffident secretary. Shut *up*. I know light is incoherent.
Look, branches inflate, unfold, at evening &

I suck my marvelous thumb.

Soul Pressure

A picture is all I have. All I have ever wanted to give, Lord.
The trees, diminishing: a tunnel & archway.
There is a child. There is a man.
Lord, I prefer the child smoothing over the cracked leaves, carrying home color
        on his shoes.
Bringing a prayer to you, 2 or 3 words.

Small hands that are yours, Lord. Black, indecipherable, magnificent things.
That are yours. Everywhere I turn. Everywhere I turn is a detour from the soul.
The soul, a detour from the self, Lord.
The rain falling there is slow & terrific.
The boy you made, Lord, loves the rain, cool as cloth on the face.

Loves thinking of the leaves comforted. Worthy, then, of being in their presence.
The boy draws a diagram of when it opened. Fast leaves. Intersected lines, Lord,
        of course.
He is a dot. He is a scent. Compresses it. The way to you when he forgets it.
See how he has drawn you as a crown, Lord. In purple because the gold is gone.
See how much he wants you. The gate to the heart swings on its hinge. He spits on it,

with affection, so it will not squeak when he touches it.

In Autumn,

I sing, leaves falling down
in color, equal parts:
snowflake & fresco.

I sing, I got two inches
of drink too, American
flag cake burning in oven.

If poets could talk, I sing:
cover him. Lonesome?
I want I want I want lonesome.

One sentence of email *lonesome,*
sky: a buried city *lonesome.*
I sing each night

tracked with brick chip,
sea against prison wall,
I sing.

Letters we all send from hell,
look, they burn up.
World War Four: I sing,

how could we know when
we were young *lonesome.*
Cold, cover him.

(Joe Strummer 1952-2002)

6. Summer Day

The Road

We had American cooking in a diner.
It was dusk. Everyone felt
like dancing and singing.
No one did, except the drunk.

Mick had to say goodbye
to every waitress and the cook.
The cook's grief seemed real as tears in a dream.
The moon turned every fallen blossom to light.

Tomorrow?
I let my arm drift out the car window and it flew away.

A.M.

I think Death will come
when my face is wrapped
in warm towels in a barber shop.
We will exchange witty, brilliant,

noir chit-chat and comebacks in the delicious,
ambiguous moments of postponement
before the inevitable and ineffable.
I will feel rich, at last,

elegantly dressed as a mobster.
One cool customer.
I will finally have shaved this damn beard.
Until then, birdsong slits

the fabric of morning and aromatic shadows
spill on the trees and gold grass.
The coffee, black, hot, but not too hot,
the way I like it.

AUTUMN

A man dropped off a ferry.
It was a costume party,
under a full moon.
He was dressed in a wedding gown.

The lake smelled like
wind from childhood.
The lights from the ship and the blowing
decorations must have been beautiful

from there, on the black water.
The veils and fabric
saturated with the shiny, black water,
pulling him down, and he drowned.

It must have been beautiful.
It must have been like dying.

SUMMER DAY

When I consider the soul,
I am watching an open
heart surgery on television.
The surgeons, I am sure of this,

are not wearing hospital masks.
Indeed, they wear wet,
black handkerchiefs,
casually tied.

You can plainly see
their breathing.
Further, they are turned away and
looking out the window.

The scraping of one cloud across a gorgeous
summer sky, a tiny rip appearing,
a few inches, unmistakable.

Pale Blossoms

Everyone understands the bricks and the silence
and the raveling pale blossoms.
It is when the demons stay up late drinking

on the tar that has heaved and broken up
that the story becomes unclear.
The Blessed Virgin, they believe,
was driving the car trying to get away,
which is astoundingly silly.

The red chips and flakes where the kid
bounced the ball to boom-boxed
Talking Heads is a mystery.
Likely not a mystery in the exact sense,
yet it resembles a dark question enough to pass.

The way is lost when we know where we are going.
It is cumbersome, but this does help us
to withstand the turbulence and seasickness.
Who among us would rather not have a clue

about lilac, about mud, about the rats.
Even the Buddha sounds like bullshit
in the right frame of mind.

But when you pass over the bridge,
toward the movie of fire, daisy
poking from a rock, the air finally cool,
you can say *the other side* and know it is true.

Toward An Understanding Of Evening

Let me say here, *Loneliness* is a kind of cologne no one would buy.
I look down the long century of yards into the house at the corner,

where a woman is moving in a peasant dress, holding a lantern,
or a cocktail in fluorescent kitchen light.

Understand evening? I am happy to have it for moments, coated with oily light,
thrown against the wall, with fragments of tree shadow. We say *the heart breaks*.

Literally.
You are sweeping the mirror pieces, singing a gauche song:

A gauche song, but I am singing,
gauche bells, gauche night, but I am singing.

Hidden Track

The trash trucks, leaf-shredders & fall come.
A phone number gets you out of this place just so far.
River dot com, oaks. *Don't give me grief,* in other words,

in this world. Dying dot com. Totally.
I mean light, too.
Cigarette & firing squad. Stolen maps.

Blindfold & cigarette. In bed, I can be
sugar, too & ants & crumbs.
Your sugar, but you know that.

Kiss me while we're young as rock songs.
Kiss me while you're dripping & red.
Dirtypictures dot net only kisses me so far.

Acknowledgments:

Some of these poems first appeared in the following journals:

American Poetry Review: "September Evening," "Miniature II," "Dirt Floor II," "Summer Day"; *Bateau Press*: "Outline," "Imago Mundi"; *Blackbird*: "Study / Bees," "Study / Leaves," "Study / Moon"; *Clown War*: "Rain Early in September"; *Cranky*: "Loop"(I stood before . . .) (nominated for a Pushcart Prize); *CrossConnect*: "On Earth," "Loop" (The trees are . . .); *Dark Sky*: "Hunger"; *Elixir* (and *Philadelphia Inquirer* online): "Pale Blossoms"; *Endicott Review*: "Mystery"; *Fox Chase Review*: "Soul Pressure"; *Frisson*: "Untitled," "Hell"; *Hinge*: "Notebook"; *Mad Poets Review*: "Hymn," "December," "Autumn," "Study / Field" (Awarded 2005 Mad Poets First Prize, selected by Gerald Stern); *Mudfish*: "Email" (Awarded 2007 Mudfish First Prize, selected by David Lehman, nominated for a Pushcart Prize); *New Zoo Review*: "Escaping in America" (nominated for a Pushcart Prize); *On and On Screen*: "Toward an Understanding of Evening"; *Philadelphia Poets*: "For Now," "Late October"; *Philadelphia Stories*: "A.M.," "The Road" (also published in *The Best of Philadelphia Stories II*); *Poet Lore*: "Incoming Prayer"; *P.F.S. Post*: "Autumn Sonata," "Apprenticeship," "April"; *Pool*: "Twenty Lines for j"; *Press 1*: "Worst Enemy" (also published in *The Red Room: Writings From Press 1*); *Prick of the Spindle*: "Study / Scarlet," "Study / Violet" (also published in *Dwarf Stars Science Fiction Anthology*); *QND Review*: "Voice"; *Rattle*: "Falling," "Redemption / Salvation"; *Schuylkill Valley Journal*: "Complete Zen Writings," "Autumn in The World"; *Scythe*: "Etude 3," "Airports and Trees"; *Shadowtrain*: "The Summer," "Orpheus in His Underwear," "063," "Reading Circle Jerk"; *Unpleasant Event Schedule*: "Two Philosophical Models."

The title of this book comes from a song by Jimmy Scott on his CD *Heaven*, written by Joyce Rambo.